Lean Startup

Step-by-Step Guide To Lean Startup

(Methodology and Models)

Jason Bennett & Jennifer Bowen

TABLE OF CONTENTS

Introduction

I want to thank you for choosing this book, 'Lean Startup'

The lean startup method is a tool that transforms a startup into a structured organization. The lean startup gives an entrepreneur a scientific approach to help him or her create and manage a startup to develop a product that the customer wants faster.

This method teaches every aspiring entrepreneur how he or she can begin a startup, what drives the startup, how to steer, how and when to turn when it is necessary to persevere and what must be done to accelerate the business. This method provides a set of principles that help the startup grow into a sustainable company.

There are many startups that start with the idea of developing a product that they believe their customers want. They spend days, weeks, months and years to perfect the product they have in mind without showing the product to the customer.

Since they do not show the product to their customers, there is a higher probability of failure than success. Besides starting a business may seem a little intimidating but it depends on the way you go about it.

There are a few aspects you need to consider if you want to build a lean startup. This book contains all the information you would need to begin a lean startup. Over the course of the book, you will learn what the principles of a lean startup are and how those principles help a startup become a sustainable organization.

The steps charted out in the book are based on the well-known Lean Startup method that was explained by Eric Ries. This book acts as a guide and takes you through the journey of a lean startup in a simple and easy manner.

Thank you once again for choosing the book. I hope you find it informative and interesting.

Chapter One: The Lean Startup Methodology

Eric Ries said that startups could be a success if they follow a certain process. This means that the process can always be learned and those who have experience can also teach them. Every entrepreneur will always wonder whether a startup will fail.

If you wish to begin a lean startup, you must identify a small gap in the market using time and money effectively. You will need to use different techniques to ensure that your product or service reaches the market in a faster way while also avoiding the production or manufacture of products that no consumer will want.

Most amateur entrepreneurs feel that they are taking a shot in the dark when they are identifying a product or service they can offer to their potential consumers.

But, it does not always have to be a trial and error proposition. If you adapt lean thinking, you will be able to develop ideas and refine them to meet market standards.

Let me show you some principles that will give a start-up a greater chance of making a profit and becoming a success within a limited budget.

Principles of Lean Start-Up

Controlled Use and Deployment of Resources

One of the most important principles of a lean startup is that the startup must use every one of its resources effectively and efficiently. Since most startups do not have enough investment they use the lean business model to encourage the effective deployment and continuous development of the resources that the company does have.

A lean startup must continuously evaluate how the initial investment can be used to meet their targets and their customer requirements.

The startup must also ensure that it does not spend more than what is necessary to test, evaluate and refine its products. If the costs are kept at a minimum, the startup can maximize its profits whenever there is a sale.

Every lean startup is dependent on organic growth since it does not have huge capital investment.

When the profits made at the early stages are reinvested in the company, the startup can scale its operations up in a controlled manner without sacrificing quality. This is commonly called innovation accounting. This is covered in detail in the following chapter.

Entrepreneurs are everywhere

Eric Ries believes that every individual in the world is an entrepreneur. There are some successful entrepreneurs who have built their organization in their garage. You can find entrepreneurs in Hollywood, in the IRS and even in well-established organizations. These people are always looking for a way to develop products that increase value to the customer.

Entrepreneurship is management

It is important to remember that every startup is not defined by its products but is an institution. Therefore, there must be a management team in place to understand and develop the startup. This is covered in further detail in the later chapters of the book.

Validated Learning

A startup does not exist only to build products for the customers or to make money. It exists only when the management learns how to build a sustainable business. The learning can be validated through statistic measures by running experiments that test the startups' vision. This concept is covered in further detail in the next chapter.

Innovation Accounting

A startup must focus on the following to improve outcomes and also hold every entrepreneur accountable:

- How can progress be measured
- How can milestones be set
- How can work be prioritized

This requires a new type of accounting for startups, which is covered in the next chapter.

Build-Measure-Learn

Every startup looks for ways to convert its ideas into a product or service and measure how its customers receive that product or service.

When they understand the response, they will understand whether they need to pivot or persevere. This process is covered in further detail in the next chapter.

Chapter Two: Lean Startup Models

The lean startup model was introduced in the year 2011, and its impact on the economy has been enormous. The book written by Eric Ries gained immense publicity, and many companies use the information in the book to develop their startups.

However, the ideas in the book are not new; these ideas have been forgotten by most entrepreneurs since success is always measured in numbers in the business world. The methods and ideas in the book are valuable to startups as well as well-established organizations.

In his book, Eric Ries has defined a startup as a human institution whose goal is to create a new service or product under uncertain conditions. This chapter covers some of the common methods used by lean startups to design products and services of great value for the customer.

Build-Measure-Learn

The way different companies pursue innovation in today's market has been affected by the idea of using certain scientific or statistical methods to handle or calculate uncertainty.

This means that the company must define a hypothesis, build a product or service to test that hypothesis, use that product or service and learn what happens and finally adjust the attributes of the product or service to increase the value for customers.

The Build-Measure-Learn methodology can be applied to almost anything. You do not have to use this methodology to test new products alone.

You can also test a management review process, customer service idea, new features to existing products or website offers and tests. You have to carry out a test and validate the initial hypothesis to ensure that you have enough data to assess the value of the product to the customer.

The aim of every company should be to move through this methodology quickly. You have to identify if the product or service developed is worth going through another cycle or if you should come up with a new idea.

This means that you must define a specific idea that you want to test with minimum criteria that can be used for measurement. When it comes to products, you have to test whether your customers want to purchase your product or if they need it. You have to learn what your customers want and not trust what they think or say they want.

First of all you should need to ask yourself certain questions before trying an idea to see if it works. What problems does your target market have? Once you can pinpoint the problem, then you can look for solutions. Most likely, you will not find any market without faults. There are plenty of problems that need to be resolved. Even the competition cannot resolve every issue out there.

You have to have a passion about it for one thing, and you want to give them something that will resolve an issue they may have. This issue can be from something they bought somewhere else, or it can be an issue they have had for a period of time and need a solution for it.

There may not even be a problem, so it may just come down to differentiating your product from the rest.

Minimal Viable Product (MVP)

A traditional company will first have to define the specifications of every product it wants to produce or manufacture and then assess the significant cost and time that will be invested to produce that product.

The lean startup methodology encourages every startup to build the required amount of product through one loop of the Build-Measure-Learn Loop. If the company can identify such a product, it becomes the minimal viable product. This product is manufactured or developed using minimal effort and less development time.

Every startup does not necessarily have to write a code to automate processes to create an MVP. An MVP could be as simple as a slide deck or design mockups.

You have to ensure that you run these products by your customers to get enough validation to pass this product through the next cycle.

Validated Learning

Every startup must test or validate a hypothesis with the right idea in mind – learn from what is observed. There are times when startups have focused on vanity metrics that made them believe that they were indeed making progress.

This is not the right approach since you must always look at metrics that will give you some insight on the product and how it can be changed to increase its value to the customers. For example, the number of accounts opened on Instagram is a vanity metric for that platform.

The actual metric would be the number of hours spent scrolling through Instagram by each account holder. This will give the developers the true value of the product.

In the book Lean Startup, Eric Ries has provided an example of his own. A company called IMVU always showed a chart that painted a good picture to its management and investors. Many registrations were being made every single day.

However, this graph did not show if the customers or users value the service. The graph did not show the costs that went into marketing to acquire new users. This chart only looked at vanity metrics and was not designed to test a hypothesis.

Innovation Accounting

Through innovation accounting, a startup can prove that it is learning to grow and sustain as a business. A company can do this in the following ways.

Establish a baseline

The startup can run an MVP test and collect data that will enable it to set some benchmark points. You can use a smoke test where you can market the product or service you want to offer and assess your customers' interests.

This includes a sign-up form to understand if the customers want to purchase the product or service. Using that information, you can set the baseline for the first iteration of the Build-Measure-Learn Cycle. It is alright to make mistakes or have low numbers since that will help you improve.

Tuning the Product

Once the baseline has been established, you should identify one change that must be made to the product and test that improvement. Do not make all the changes at once, as it can lead to chaos.

You can try to see how a change in the design of the form attracts more customers when compared to the earlier design. This step must be carried out slowly to ensure that every hypothesis is tested out carefully.

Persevere or Pivot

When you have made several iterations through the cycle, you have to move up from the initial baseline towards the goal that was set out in the business plan. If you are unable to reach that goal, you must learn why using the data collected at every step.

Pivot

A successful entrepreneur is one who has the foresight, the tools and the ability to identify which parts of the business plan are indeed working for the company. They also learn to adapt to changes in the market and their strategies according to the data collected during the iterations.

One of the hardest aspects of the lean startup method is to make the decision to pivot since every entrepreneur and founder is emotionally attached to the product they have created. They spend a lot of money and energy to get to where they are.

If a team uses vanity metrics to test its products and hypothesis, it can go down the wrong path. If the hypothesis selected is not defined clearly, then it is possible that the company may fail since the management does not know that the endeavor is not working.

If you, as the management, decide to launch the product fully in the market and then assess the outcome, you will see what happens, and there is a higher probability that you may fail.

If you choose to pivot, it does not mean that you have failed. It means that you will change the hypothesis that you started out with. The following variations are often used when a startup chooses to pivot.

- Zoom-in Pivot: A single feature in the product that sets it apart from other products becomes the actual product.
- Zoom-out pivot: This is the opposite of the above definition where an entire product is used as a new feature in a larger product.
- Customer segment pivot: The product designed was correct. However, the customers that were selected were wrong for the product. The startup can change the customer segment and sell the same product.
- Customer need pivot: When the startup follows the principles of validated learning, it will identify the problem that needs to be solved for the customer who was initially selected.
- Platform pivot: most platforms start off as applications. When the platform becomes a success, it transforms into a platform ecosystem.
- Business Architecture Pivot: Based on Geoffrey Moore's idea, the startup can choose to switch to low margin and high-volume products from high margin and low-value products.

- Value Capture Pivot: When you decide to measure the value differently, you will be able to change everything about the business right from the cost structure to the final product.
- The engine of Growth Pivot: According to Ries, most startups follow a paid, viral or sticky growth model. It would be more prudent for the company to switch from one model to the other to grow faster.
- Channel Pivot: In today's world, advertising channels and complex sales have reduced since the Internet provides a huge platform for a company to advertise its products.
- Technology Pivot: Technological advancements are being made every day, and any new technology can help to reduce the cost and increase performance and efficiency.

Small Batches

There is a story where a father had asked his daughters to help him stuff newsletters into a document. The children suggested that they fold every newsletter, put a stamp on the envelope and write the address on the envelope.

They wanted to do every task one step at a time. The father wanted to do it differently – he suggested that they finish every envelope fully before they moved on to the next envelope.

The father and daughters competed with each other to see which the better method was.

The father's method won since he used an approach called "single-piece flow" which is common in lean manufacturing. It is better to repeat a task over and over again to ensure that you master that task. You will also learn to do the task faster and better.

You have to remember that an individual's performance is not as important as the performance of the system. You lose time when you should go back to the first task and restack the envelopes. If you consider the process as a unit, you will be able to improve your efficiency.

Another benefit of using small batches is that you will be able to spot the error immediately. If you fold all the newsletters and then find out that that newsletter does not fit into the envelope, you will need to fold all the newsletters again.

This approach will help you identify the error at the beginning and improve your process.

The advantage of working with small batches is that you will be able to identify the problems soon.

Andon Cord

The Andon Cord is a method that was used by Taiichi Ohno in Toyota, which allowed an employee to stop the process if he or she identified a defect in the process. If the defect continues longer in the process, it is harder to remove that defect, and there is a higher cost involved.

It is highly efficient to spot the defect at an early stage even if it means that the process will need to stop to address the defect. This method has helped Toyota maintain high quality.

Eric Ries mentioned in his book that the company IMVU used a set of checks that ran every day to check if the site worked accurately. This meant that they were able to identify and address any production error quickly and automatically.

There were no changes made to the production until the defect was addressed. This was an automated Andon Cord.

Continuous Deployment

Continuous deployment is a scenario that is unimaginable and scary for most startups. The idea of this method is that the startup must update the production systems regularly.

IMVU was regularly updating its production system by running close to fifty updates. This was made possible since they made an investment in test scripts. Over 14000 test scripts would run at least 60 times a day and simulate everything from a click on the browser to running the code in the database.

Eric Ries also talks about Wealthfront, which is a company that operates in an environment regulated by the SEC. However, this company practices continuous deployment and has more than ten production releases a day.

Kanban

Kanban is a technique that was borrowed from the world of lean manufacturing. It was developed by Taiichi Ohno in the late 1980s to improve the manufacturing unit of Toyota automobiles. Eric Ries mentions the company Grockit, which is an online tool that helps one build skills for standardized tests.

This tool creates a story in the development process, which is then used to develop a feature. They also mention to the user what the outcome or benefit of the tool is. These stories are validated to see how they work for different users.

A test is conducted to see how this tool benefits the customer. There are four states:

- Backlog: The tasks that can be worked on but have not yet been started
- In Progress: The tasks that are currently being developed
- Built: The tasks that have been completed and are ready for the customer
- Validated: Products that have been released and have been validated by the customers.

If the story fails the validation test, then it will be removed from the product and produced again. A good practice would be to ensure that none of the buckets mentioned above have more than two projects at a given time.

If there is a project or task that is in the built bucket, it cannot move to the validated stage until there is enough room for it. The same goes for the processes that are in the backlog bucket. These tasks cannot move to the "In Progress" bucket until it is free.

A valuable outcome of this method is that the team can start measuring its productivity based on the validated learning and feedback from the customer. The team will then stop measuring its productivity based on the number of new features developed.

The Five Whys

Every technical defect or issue has a human cause at its root. The five whys technique will allow the startup to get closer to the root cause. This is a deceptively simple technique but is powerful.

Eric Ries has mentioned in his book that most problems or issues that are identified in a process are caused due to lack of training. These problems may look like an individual's mistake or a technical issue. Ries uses IMVU as an example to explain this technique.

- A new product feature or release was disabled for customers. Why? The feature tanked because of a failed server.
- Why did this server fail? There was a subsystem that was used incorrectly.
- Why was that server used incorrectly? The engineer using the server was not trained to use it properly.
- Why did he not know how to use the server? He was never trained.
- Why was he not trained? His manager did not believe that new engineers needed to be trained since he believed that he and his team were too busy.

This technique is extremely useful for startups since it helps them make improvements within a short period. A huge amount can be invested in training, but this may not be the optimal thing to do when the startup is still at its development stage.

If the startup takes a look at the root cause of every problem, it can identify the core areas that need to be worked on and not focus only on the issues at the surface.

Most people tend to overreact to issues that happen at the moment, and the Five Whys help them understand what they need to look at to understand what is happening. There is a possibility that the Five Whys can be used as a way to blame people in the team to see whose fault it was. The goal of this method is to identify problems that are caused not by bad people but by bad processes.

It is essential that every member of the team be in the same room when this analysis is made. When blame needs to be taken, it is important that the management should take the hit for not having a solution at system-level. Good practices to follow to get started with this methodology are:

- Mutual empowerment and trust. If a mistake is made for the first time, you should be tolerant of them. Ensure that you do not make the same mistake twice.
- Maintain focus on the system since most mistakes happen due to a flaw in the system and ensure that people always solve problems at the system level.
- The company should always face some unpleasant truths. This method will bring out some unpleasant truths to the surface, and the management should ensure that these issues are taken care of at the initial stage. If this method is not conducted in the right manner, it will change into the Five Blames.
- Always start small and be specific. You have to look at the process in detail and always start with small issues. When you understand the issues, you must identify the solutions. Always run the process regularly and involve as many people from the team as you can.
- Appoint someone who is a master at Five Whys. This person must be the primary change agent and should have a good degree of authority to ensure that things get done. This person

will be accountable for judging whether the costs were made to prevent or work on those problems are paying off or not.

The Five Whys methodology is used to transform the startup into a more organized and adaptive organization, which can be hard.

Chapter Three: How to Envision the Startup

When you build a startup, you have to know where to start which means that you will need to create a team that oversees the management of the startup. You will also need to learn to define your product and startup to help customers understand why your product is different from the other products in the market.

Ensure that your learning is incorporated into the product and experiment with different ideas before you launch your product in the market.

Start – Entrepreneurship is management

When you build a startup, you build an institution, which needs to be managed. This may come as a surprise to some entrepreneurs since they believe that there is no correlation between management and startup.

It is good that most entrepreneurs are wary of setting up a traditional management system since it can stifle creativity and invite bureaucracy.

Entrepreneurs in different industries have been trying to look for solutions to their problems in traditional management for quite some time which leads to the "just do it" attitude. These entrepreneurs avoid all forms of discipline, management and process.

What they forget is that this attitude leads to failure more often than it does success. It must be remembered that the principles of general management are not well suited to handle failure or chaos that every startup must face.

Every startup must have some level of managerial discipline to ensure that the company can harness all the opportunities it has been given. There are many entrepreneurs today when compared to any other time in history, which has been made possible due to globalization. For example, most news channels and radio stations have commented about how people are losing jobs in the manufacturing industry.

However, the manufacturing output of every company has increased over the last decade, which means that modern technology and management have helped to improve productivity.

If you wish to build a lean startup, you should consider entrepreneurial management since it encourages employees to expand their horizons and knowledge. Consider the following situation – there is an established company with a team that has not made any sales in over a year.

This department has not roped in new customers either. However, the employees in that department have identified a new industry or line of business the company can diversify its assets into. In an established organization, the department would be dissolved since the company is always looking for ways to make a profit. However, in entrepreneurial management, these employees are considered entrepreneurs since they are looking for ways to improve the business.

Define

If you ever go for an entrepreneur meet, you will notice that many people have no idea what is expected of them. You will find a group of traditional entrepreneurs and managers from well-established companies who are expected to create product innovations or ventures.

These managers are good at organizational politics and know how the company can be divided into groups and how the profit and loss for each department can be separated. The surprising thing is that these individuals are visionaries since they can see the future of their company and are prepared to take risks to find innovative and new solutions to any problem the company faces.

Entrepreneurs who work in an organization are called intrapreneurs since they work on products or build a startup within the organization. Intrapreneurs have a lot in common with entrepreneurs.

The lean startup method is a set of principles and practices that every entrepreneur can use to build a successful startup. It was mentioned earlier that Eric Ries defined a startup as a human institution that is designed to develop a new product or service under uncertain conditions. This definition omits the industry, sector of the economy and the size of the business.

Most people lose sight of the fact that a startup is a brilliant idea, product or a breakthrough apart from being a human institution. Additionally, it is a product or service defined as an innovation.

It is important that the word innovation is understood in a broad sense. Every startup uses a different kind of innovation to increase value to its customer.

It is also important for the startup to understand the conditions under which innovation happens. Startups enter an industry where there is an established organization that already sells the same product.

They must find a new attribute to the product that has not been sold to the customers before developing it. The development stage is uncertain since the product could either be accepted or rejected by the customer.

Learn

Every entrepreneur must make an effort to learn and understand whether the company was indeed making progress. Many entrepreneurs develop a product using their creativity, and they launch that product in the market. If the product fails at the market, they believe they have learned why and they go ahead and develop a better product. Unfortunately, this is the oldest excuse for failure.

These entrepreneurs become wildly creative about what they have learned from their failure. However, this is not comforting for employees or investors since the former are giving the startup their time while the latter have allotted their money to the startup.

An entrepreneur cannot go to a bank and tell them that he or she has learned what needs to be done to sell the product in the market. It is no wonder the word learning has a bad name in the market.

It is important that every startup learns how a product can be improved and also understands what needs to be done better to succeed. The previous chapter lists a few methods that can be used to help an entrepreneur learn.

Experiment

When an entrepreneur has an idea in mind, he or she will want to find a way to execute that idea. Every startup is built in the hopes that the entrepreneur has identified a product or service that does not exist in the market and will increase value to its customers.

A mistake that most entrepreneurs make is that they launch the product on the market before they test it. There is a high probability that this product or service may not appeal to the customers.

Therefore, it becomes important that the startup launches the product to a smaller audience and gathers feedback before launching the product in the market. This gives the entrepreneur the chance to tweak the product to increase value to the customer.

Chapter Four: How to Steer

When you have identified your product and developed it, you will launch it in the market and ask your customers to use it. You must remember that there is a possibility of a failure. But, do not worry too much since you can learn from that failure and develop a better product.

Leap

Every entrepreneur must have the ability to take a leap of faith and make a risky decision about his or her idea. There are two types of assumptions that can be made – Value Hypothesis and Growth Hypothesis.

Value Hypothesis

How can you as an entrepreneur validate every assumption you have made about your product's value? It depends on how quickly you can develop a prototype and give your customers the chance to use that prototype and give you feedback. You do not necessarily have to give the main product to the customers.

You can do what Zomato did. Deepinder Goyal saw that people had trouble waiting in a queue for food. Instead, they launched a website that had scanned copies of menus which enabled people to decide their order before they stepped into the line. When this became a success, they developed Zomato and roped in more restaurants and cafes.

Growth Hypothesis

You must focus on the growth of your company only when you have an established product. You have to ask yourself how customers will use your product constantly. The best way to do this would be to ask the customers for feedback. Facebook and WhatsApp are great examples.

Test

When you use the minimum viable product (MVP) approach, you will learn more about how the product can be improved. An MVP is not a small product, and it is simply a faster way to complete one iteration of the build-measure-learn cycle.

This has been mentioned in the previous chapter. You have to remember that your first product does not have to be perfect. It should be a rough idea of what you had in mind and then test that idea with your customers and gather feedback.

You must ensure that through this test, you can validate your initial hypothesis.

There are different tests that can be conducted to understand how the customers received the product.

Quantitative versus qualitative

There is a constant debate to understand which is superior. It is a good approach to first use qualitative research and assesses the feedback before validating a hypothesis using the quantitative approach.

Generative versus Evaluative

The former can be used to test the product if there is no hypothesis in place. The latter is where a hypothesis is tested to understand whether or not the product is a success or failure. If you do not have a clear hypothesis, you should use the generative approach to either obtain new ideas or to develop a particular hypothesis.

Market versus Product

There are some situations where the market will give you an idea of what the customers want. All you need to do is listen to the customers and understand what problems they face. There are other situations where a product or service must be developed to solve a problem.

Measure

Every startup is a more than just a piece of paper. The initial business plan will list out the number of customers the company expects to have, the cost it will incur and the revenue or profit it will make.

This plan is usually far from where the startup is in the early days. Therefore, it is important that a startup works on the following:

- It must identify where the startup is right now by accepting the truth that is revealed through constant assessment.
- Devise new experiments to understand how the startup can move towards the numbers mentioned in the business plan.

Most products, including the ones that fail, have some growth, positive results and customers. As an entrepreneur, you will be optimistic and will trust the ideas that you have. This does not mean that you can bumble around and be happy with the little traction that you have. You should ensure that you do not persevere when things do not go your way.

Persevere or Pivot

The second chapter of the book talks about how an entrepreneur can pivot. When one says pivot, it does not mean that they should give up on their ideas. There are different ways that an entrepreneur can still make his or her product work. Try the methods mentioned above to help you when you reach the pivot stage.

If every test and experiment conducted gives you the best results, you should develop the product fully and launch it in the market. Ensure that you do not trick yourself by using vanity measures to test your hypothesis.

Always use criteria that will affect your company to assess the products that you are developing. You must also ensure that you listen to your customers and understand their wants and needs better.

You have to remember that a startup's productivity is not measured by adding more features to a product.

It is about how the startup aligns its efforts with a product or business to drive growth and create value. If you learn how to pivot successfully, you can reach the path of sustainable business growth.

Chapter Five: How to Accelerate

Most decisions that need to be made by a startup are not clear or straightforward. They have to constantly question their product and assess when it can be launched in the market. They have to also look at how the product should be released and the cost that they will incur.

Batch

There is a small example in the second chapter about how a father and his two daughters competed with each other to stuff newsletters into envelopes. The issues mentioned in that example are found in every process in an organization, and they are of greater consequence in the work of small or large companies.

Some companies use a large-batch approach where they develop and deliver all the products at the end of the process and at once. Other companies use a small-batch approach where it produces and delivers a finished product every few minutes.

A big advantage of working in small batches is that problems in the product can be identified faster. Lean manufacturing discovered small-batch processing a few decades ago when Taiichi Ohno and Shigeo Shingo worked to enhance the productivity of Toyota Automobiles. They started to manufacture products one at a time and stopped any activity if there was a defect in the process.

Once the defect was removed, the product was manufactured in small batches. This gave Toyota the ability to produce diverse products.

They gathered that every product can be different and does not have to be produced in bulk. This allowed them to serve smaller customer segments and give the customers products that they needed.

Grow

There are times when a startup can have customers at early stages and good revenue at that stage. However, the company may stop growing in the sense that it continues to make the same revenue and has the same number of customers now that it had at its start.

So, where does growth stem from? A company can only grow if new customers are brought into it, which can only be done by the action of all its past customers. There are four ways to obtain new customers:

- A startup can use the Internet to advertise its products and services. Most businesses do this to encourage new customers to buy their products. If you want this to be a successful venture, you should pay for advertising through your revenue and not out of the initial capital.
- New customers can be brought through the use of products. For example, if a customer sees someone wearing new clothes, he or she may want to purchase similar clothing. The same can be said about cars and bikes. This is also true for products like PayPal and Instagram.
- If a customer is satisfied with the product or service provided by the company, he or she will spread the word and encourage more people to purchase that product.
- There are some products that need to be repeatedly purchased. If you develop such a product, you can create a subscription plan that ensures that customers keep coming back to you.

Adapt

It is important for a startup to adapt for change. Every employee in the startup should constantly be trained. Some people working in traditional organizations may tell you that you should not spend too much money on training when you are a startup. This is bad advice since it is important to train every employee in the organization to help them develop new ideas. It has become evident that technology is going to take over many jobs in the near future.

This does not mean that someone should sit tight and continue with their work and not develop their skills. It is important that they learn new skills or programming languages that will give them an edge. New jobs can be created to cater to these new skills.

The same can be said for a startup. It must constantly evolve its products and develop new products or services that will appeal to the customers.

As an entrepreneur, you should be strong and deal with negative comments or feedback. You must learn from that feedback and develop products that will add value to the customers.

Use the Five Whys technique to help you understand what your customers want and why the initial prototype of your product failed in the market. You also have to learn to start small. Do not begin with four or five hypotheses. Start off with one hypothesis and test that with the data collected from the customers.

You must ensure that you do not blame an individual or a team for failure since that brings the morale of the employees down. Accept that mistakes do happen and learn from them.

Innovate

Innovation is the key to a bright future for any company. It is believed that when companies become large, they lose the ability to innovate. However, this is a myth that has been bringing many companies and employees down.

When a startup is growing, it will test its products in the market and find ways to make the product better to appeal to its customers. It will also need to find new attributes to add to the existing product to generate new customers. This is innovation since the company is looking for ways to enhance the existing product.

If a well-established organization is willing to change its management, it can also start innovating. Innovation teams must be built to ensure that a company succeeds. This is what keeps Apple apart from all other companies.

Apple is one company that has always developed new versions of its devices to meet customer demands. The developers include new features into the code every few months to generate a new product. Apple has also ensured that its products are user-friendly and can sustain bad handling.

Most customers have confirmed that an Apple laptop has a firewall that makes it difficult for any virus to penetrate. This is the kind of product that you should develop. Ensure that you constantly innovate and make your products better to meet your customers' demands. Remember to listen to the customers and make informed decisions about what the customers need. Customers are not sure of what they want or need on most occasions.

They believe that they know what they want, but in reality, they use the products that have great reviews. It is important that you pay attention to what your customers want before you develop a product or make changes to an existing product.

Conclusion

Thank you for purchasing the book.

Eric Ries defined the lean startup methodology in his book "Lean Startup." Most startups fail in the initial stages since they cannot grasp hard truths. There are many startups that have succeeded, Facebook being a prime example.

They succeeded because they constantly kept in touch with the customers and assessed what the customers wanted or needed by the company. The lean startup method follows the same principles.

Over the course of this book, you will gather information on what the lean startup methodology is and how this method should be applied by entrepreneurs to ensure that the startup becomes a sustainable organization.

The principles outlined in the book will help you understand how a startup must be built to meet a customer's needs and demands. This book acts as a guide for those who want to build a lean startup and have a good product in mind.

If you follow the steps mentioned in the book word for word, you will succeed in your venture.

I hope you have gathered all the information you were looking for and wish you luck on your journey!

www.ingramcontent.com/pod-product-compliance
Lightning Source LLC
Chambersburg PA
CBHW071153220526
45468CB00003B/1035